BUILDING A GET HOME BAG

TIPS FOR SETTING UP A REALISTIC BUG OUT BAG FOR GETTING BACK HOME IN A DISASTER

DAVID NASH

CONTENTS

PREFACE

Since you are reading a book on self-reliance, I am assuming you want to know more about how to take care of yourself in disaster situations

I would like to suggest you take a moment and visit my website and YouTube channel for thousands of hours of free content related to basic preparedness concepts

Dave's Homestead Website
https://www.tngun.com

Dave's Homestead YouTube Channel
https://www.youtube.com/tngun

Shepherd Publishing
https://www.shepherdpublish.com

1
____

INTRODUCTION

A bugout bag/72 hour kit is one of the very first projects a new prepper makes as they explore the idea of becoming more self-reliant. A quick search for the term "bug out bag" on Amazon kindle shows more than 9 pages of books. Why should you read this one?

I can only explain why by telling you my own personal ideas on the subject. With very few exceptions, the "experts" in prepping are all just selling you their own ideas and personal bias. Most of us teach what we believe, but are not a lot of writers in this subject that have lived through a grid down or other catastrophic disaster, so as I said, its all personal ideas.

While it is true that I haven't lived through a Zombie Apocalypse, I have a unique set of skills. I have been a personal preparedness advocate since I led a school-wide new Madrid preparation program as a High School Freshman. After the Marines, and a few years working inside various state prisons, I began working in state level emergency management. I have a degree in Emergency Management, and worked for over a decade in preparedness planning, training, and operations at the State level. I know exactly how the government will react and what they are prepared to do. I also understand the prepper mindset, as I have been one since junior high school.

This book is similar in scope to my 21 Days to Basic Preparedness[1] ebook in that it explores personal preparations from the viewpoint of the modern science of emergency management. In this short work I will discuss the fundamental differences in types of emergency kits and bags. However, this work focuses on the specifics of a Get Home Bag rather than a more general bug out bag. I also hope to help you build a kit that will actually be useful rather than something that may get you in trouble or be too heavy to carry.

I have worked in emergency management during some very serious disasters. I was in charge of the Logistical Support Area for the May 2010 Nashville Floods, worked support during Katrina, and during my time in Operations I participated in hundreds of smaller scale local disasters and emergency response activities. I have even worked a nuclear plant emergency response once or twice. From that experience, I know the work and thought that goes into running a shelter during a disaster. Emergency management workers try very hard to make shelters safe and comfortable. However, the lack of privacy, resources, and independence makes me pretty hesitant to choose to go to a shelter as long as I have other options.

Personally, it would take a very severe reason for me to

evacuate or "bug out" from my home in the first place. Leaving the house would entail me having to leave many of my in-place systems and make me more vulnerable to outlaws and well meaning (and otherwise) bureaucrats.

However, just because I don't WANT to evacuate from my homestead doesn't mean I won't HAVE to evacuate. I don't want any kind of disaster to befall my family, but measuring risk says I should be prepared "just in case".

While, my goal is to not have to bug out, I can see lots of situations where I would need to "get home"

Before we get into the necessity to have a special kit in your vehicle that will help you "get home". There is a need to discuss the various types of emergency kits. However, buying a bag of stuff won't help if you don't have the skills and mindset to use them. In my experience, both as a prepper, and an emergency manager, I find that before you should buy things you should develop the right skills.

2

PERSONAL PREPAREDNESS MINDSET

Personal preparedness means different things depending on who you are and what your situation is. To an inhabitant of the Florida Keys, preparedness means having items to outlast a hurricane. To a city dweller, preparedness might be having a can of mace in her purse. To a survivalist, preparedness might mean having a semi trailer loaded with M14 rifles buried in the back yard. Depending on the situation, any of these definitions might be appropriate. Whatever your situation, cultivating a personal preparedness mindset is the key to thriving in times of adversity.

Personal preparedness is simply knowing what dangers are likely to befall you and taking reasonable precautions to avoid or survive them. In today's modern world, insurance is a required item. No one laughs at a car owner that buys a full coverage policy for his or her car. As a matter of fact, a driver that fails to insure their car is looked upon as irresponsible, sometimes even criminal. The same

thing can be said about homeowner's or renter's insurance, life insurance, and health insurance. Today people
take out money for retirement in the form of IRA's,
401K's, mutual funds and the like. No one faults them.
Why is it that someone who has a pantry of stored food,
candles, a rifle or two, and ammunition for them is
considered crazy or dangerous? Isn't it a logical extension
of the doctrine of insurance? After all insurance is merely
a device to lessen the extent a disaster has on your life. If
having an extra insurance policy for break-ins is smart,
then the idea of someone breaking into your home is
possible. If it is likely that someone might break into
your home, then having a means to protect yourself is
justified.

Each year natural disasters occur in the United States.
When these occur, the news media rushes to the scene. It
never fails that they show a relief organization van at the
disaster site. Usually there is an interview with someone
who is standing in line looking for help. The site is
common; a desperate parent with a hungry child waiting
for someone to give them some milk for their infant.
Ratings soar and people feel sorry for this poor child.
Consider this, areas prone to natural disaster are known.
Floods happen on a regular basis. Places like Tornado
Alley have been recognized and named. If the choice is
made to live in an area like this and the basic precautions
are not taken, then pity is not the logical emotion. Irre-
sponsibility on the part of the parent caused the child's
pain; it only takes a few extra seconds to grab a couple
extra bottles of formula. Why didn't they take this simple
precaution? They probably paid the cable bill. Does that

expense outweigh the measly cost of a gallon of Bottled water?

Organizations like the American Red Cross and the Office of Homeland Security suggest that each family has a few days of essential items[1] to get them through an emergency. Doing this is not hard nor does it have to be expensive. No one says that preparedness means having a years supply of freeze dried steak in a concrete storage bunker. Simply buying a can or two of extra food every time you go shopping is enough. Buy an extra box of garbage bags, some extra toilet tissue, or any item you have to have. Store it in a box under the bed, or in the closet. In hardly any time at all, you will soon have a store pile that will give you not only an added measure of security, but also a sense of well-being. Rotate this stock out. As you eat a box of macaroni, buy another. Forget that you have four boxes on your kitchen shelf. This causes you not to feel over burdened financially to support your prepared lifestyle. It also keeps your store fresh. An added benefit is that your safety net is familiar to you. In the stressful time of disaster, you don't have the added stressor of eating unfamiliar foods chosen not by your appetite, but by their shelf life.

It is easy to lecture on what items are needed. Lists of essential items depend on lifestyle and location as much as physical needs. It would be irresponsible to dictate what equipment your family would need to survive without knowing you or your situation. You must sit down and decide what your family's priorities are, and from that list determine your family's needs.

It is not important what others say or think of you. It is not even recommended to tell your neighbors you find the need to be prepared for life. Does it matter if they think you are crazy for stockpiling groceries? Will it matter if your children or spouse suffer because you want to keep the good graces of the people 2 doors down?

TYPES OF EMERGENCY KITS

Any prepper or interested party with access to the internet has probably noticed the love of acronyms as they relate to kits and gear. You have: BOB, INCH, GOOD, GHB, and EDC, IFAK, 72 hour kits, and 1st 2nd and 3rd line gear. The confusion just piles on.

Basically, the name of the kit relates to its usage. It is a way to pack items together to help you survive an incident as well as describe the philosophy that caused you to pack it all together.

Back during my podcasting days, one of my most popular episodes dealt with an introduction to prepper kits[1].

Basically it all starts with the 72 hour kit, which comes from the US military and is based around the fact that American soldiers are resupplied so often that they only need to be self-sufficient for three days at a time. This level is what the US government recommends for all citizens, because in the event of a federally declared disaster it will take FEMA approximately three days to get a supply system organized to provide relief. A 72 hour kit should have basic cooking, lighting, shelter, water, and food to survive for three days.

Everyday Carry

EDC or everyday carry are things you have on you every-day. A whole prepper subset has evolved around EDC. Generally for me my EDC is a couple knives, a cell phone, a cheap screwdriver set and P-38 on my key chain, and if I am carrying my "man purse" I'll have some Altoid tins containing a sewing kit and OTC medicine, and some car charger adaptors. I would love to have a pistol in my EDC, but I now work inside a prison so that is forbidden.

Bug Out Bag

BOB, bob, or B.o.B means Bug Out Bag. A BOB is a small bag that is basically a portable 72 hour kit. The idea is that if a fire or something broke out and you had to leave RIGHT NOW, you can throw on your shoes, grab your BOB and have whatever essential medicines, food, and clothes that you would need. A good idea is to have copies of vital records in your bob, so that you won't lose them if you don't have time to dig around in your filing cabinet.

Get Out of Dodge Bag

A GOOD bag or Get out of Dodge bag, is a larger BOB,

but still small enough to pack quickly. It's pretty much interchangeable with a BOB. Some preppers have GOOD trailers or GOOD vehicles that are pre-packed. I use big plastic totes with a color code system. Each food tote contains approximately a month of food rather than a single commodity. In an emergency I can grab as many as I have room for and not have to worry about grabbing a 50 pound bucket of wheat but forgetting the salt or grinder.

I'm Never Coming Home Bag

An INCH bag on the other hand means "I'm Never Coming Home". Its more of a Mad Max/The Road/Postman type problem where you have to take what you can carry, but all you get is what you take. My inch bag would contain everything in my GOOD kit, plus extras like my hand reloading press, more tools, and reference materials.

Individual First Aid Kit / Improved First Aid Kit

IFAK is not a general preparedness kit, but it took me a minute to connect the dots so I will throw it in as a "good to know". IFAK is an improved first aid kit. It is basically a one pound kit that addresses major blood loss and airway distress. Some also call it an *individual* first aid kit.

Line Gear

Line gear is also a military concept and revolves around the gear you would need to complete a mission. It's not exactly applicable to citizen preppers, but it is related in many ways.

First Line Gear is your EDC, and focuses on what you would carry on your person. This would include your clothing, knife, weapon and maybe a small survival and first aid kit. Obviously, if you are an office worker your EDC would be much different from a law enforcement officer, or a coal miner. Don't go mall ninja on me though and carry a bunch of neato, jiffy, wow stuff to feel cool. Everything needs a use or you won't carry it all the time.'

2nd line gear is your "fighting load". When I have my "Jack Baur bag" (my wife calls it a "murse" but jack pack, messenger bag are all appropriate terms.) I can carry more prepper stuff, flashlights, hand held radio, batteries, power bars. It also can go with me almost everywhere and gives me more capability without sacrificing a lot of maneuverability. IF it was a full on WROL (without rule of law, IMHO that is VERY unlikely) this would most likely take the form of a load bearing vest, or chest rig to hold ammunition for your rifle.

3rd line gear is your pack, i.e. sustainment items you need for a longer term. Your not going to fight wearing your rucksack, you would drop it and depend on your 1st and 2nd line gear during the fight and then go back and get your pack to refill your empty magazines.

The thing is, who cares what you call your stuff, organize it to suit your needs and as long as you understand what your doing and why you are light years ahead of guys that follow the conventional prepper wisdom and build kits based upon what some internet guru wrote in a list. Your also galaxies ahead of people who haven't even given a thought to prepping.

You don't need to be scared, but it is important that you take some time to develop a plan you can work with.

4

WHAT IS A GET HOME BAG

A GHB or Get Home Bag is practically the same as a BOB, but logistically the opposite. A GHB is a portable kit containing the essentials you would need if you have to find an alternate route home if disaster struck while you were away from home. I work at a local prison, that is a 45 minute drive from my home. My wife teaches at a school 45 minutes in the opposite direction. If something were to happen during the work day we are three counties apart. How would we be able to survive, to communicate, and to get home?

If something happened and I had to leave my car and walk home, I would want a lightweight kit that allowed me to change out of my work clothes, and gave me some comfort and security on a long trek home. I keep a GHB in both mine, and my wife's vehicles because the Get Home Bag sits in a car trunk, weight is not an issue, and space is not a substantially limiting factor. However, if I have to carry the kit on my back, then weight and space most definitely is.

As backpackers and soldiers know; ounces make pounds, pounds make pain.

What I do, is keep a box with lots of related items in the trunks of the cars. Then, in a disaster, I can sort through and pick what is needed for the specifics of the event.

Space and weight are not an issue in the car, so I have things in my box that I can pick through to make a bag that best fits my situation. In many ways my GHB is actually a box that has items for light vehicle repair, minimalist camping, and an expeditious walk home.

Don't misunderstand, in a disaster, I am not going to have time to unload and pack a bag for scratch. I keep the essentials in a small day pack, and have items like a car survival/emergency kit with jumper cables, 12 volt air pump, LED road flares and spare tools.

Car Emergency Kits

Car Survival Kits are specifically designed to provide survival supplies if you are trapped in or become disabled or lost while traveling in your vehicle. Automobile emergency kits are not the same as a Survival Kit. An automobile kit generally contain flares, jumper cables, spare fuses, etc. They help the car, not you.

Most folks don't understand why a car kit is important. However, those same people can vividly recall news reports of a person pinned in their wrecked car for days.

THE REALITY OF A GET HOME BAG

True story:

The prison I work at had a random car search, and the shift "mall ninja" had to open up his car. In the back of the car they found a moss berg 590 12 gauge shotgun with the breeching barrel. Why would an employee at a prison have a shotgun in his car designed to blow hinges off doors? When asked he said it was part of his "get home kit" in the event he had to walk home. Under the shotgun was a plate carrier and chest rig to carry the spare magazines he had for the semi-automatic AK-47 clone he had stashed under the bullet proof vest. Once again, it was part of his get home kit. He also had a Glock pistol, a military molle pack, a cold steel ninja sword, a tomahawk, and 1000 rounds of various ammunition.

Looking past the size and shape of the individual and my belief he couldn't carry all his equipment a mile, much less all the way home. I am a big out of shape guy myself, so don't think I am fat shaming, but consider that a thousand rounds of anything, including .22 long rifle is heavy. So are the guns.

Besides the weight, what would you do during a disaster if you saw a corn fed crisco kid dressed out in military camouflage, carrying an AK and a sword walking through your sub-division in the middle of the night?

Many people keep firearms in their GHB's and I totally understand that, I do too. However, if you have a AR or AK platform long gun and change into a multi-cam uniform, you are going to attract unwanted attention. Consider a more concealable approach to defensive weaponry.

Personally, I want to look like Joe Sixpack with no more on me than anyone else. In a disaster I want to blend in until I have to stand out. Chances are, if you have been prepping a while, you have met someone that, in a true disaster, would murder the lone individual walking through the subdivision carrying a rifle. I bet that after shooting they individual, they would also take all of his stuff.

On top of all that, I *know* what a law enforcement official will do when spotting Paul Blart toting his arsenal during a declared State of Emergency

---

You Can't Carry Everything

The reality is, ounces make pounds, pounds make pain. You are not backpacking the Sierra Nevada Mountains, nor are you out on a long range reconnaissance patrol. The role of a get home bag is to support a fast trek home. To do this it should be lightweight, easily accessible and unobtrusive.

My GHB is stashed in a sturdy, yet older blue school book bag. On the surface it is beat up, yet it is well made. It contains items similar to what an ultra light backpacker would carry. I am not looking for comfort, I am looking for a kit to be comforting. A change of clothes that I can walk in, yet look unthreatening, broke in boots and thick socks, a pistol and 50 or so rounds in a good quality concealment holster, some food, water, and comms gear.

Unless forced, I don't plan on fighting anyone, my goal is to avoid trouble on my way home. To be honest, I don't really plan on sleeping much or doing anything more than getting home as fast as and efficiently as possible. How could I, if I have to walk home, I would be separated from my wife and son in a major disaster.

A Trunk is Not Always the Best Place for a Kit

Your supplies may be inaccessible in your trunk if you are actually trapped in your vehicle. This depends on your vehicle. For such a scenario, you'd want supplies within reach of the passenger compartment. This may not be a problem for a minivan or SUV where there is access to the entire vehicle and you or your passengers can reach the supplies.

However, sedans with a separate trunk are trickier. You could be trapped in the driver's seat and be unable to access your supplies. Although, to be fair, a scenario where you are trapped and can't get to your trunk have a very low probability of occurrence.

Although, when it is just my wife and I, I move our kit to the backseat of our car. Keeping your car survival kit in the trunk would prove effective for the majority of your scenarios. However, an extended jam could have you wishing for water. Just think about the parking lot known as Interstate 45 from Galveston to Houston any time an evacuation order is given for a hurricane!

Hot Trunks Will Reduce Storage Life

Another major consideration is shelf life in the vehicle. Car interiors get very hot in the summer, and very cold in the winter. This can wreak havoc on the storage life of your supplies.

For this reason, I use glass bottles to store my water because I don't tolerate the BPA leached from the plastic bottle into my water very well. Leaching will occur over time from any plastic water bottle, but in a hot trunk it will occur much faster. I keep a hydration bladder in my kit, but it is empty and will be filled from the glass bottles.

I have the same issue with food. I don't dislike the lemony taste of USCG approved ration bars like the Datrex, but I don't like the flaky oatmeal texture. However, of all the emergency rations I have experimented with, they have the best shelf stability in a hot car trunk.

I keep lighters stashed everywhere, the same as in my box of GHB 'stuff', in this instance I use a zippo lighter kit stored in a ziplock bag. In my kit, the lighter kit is an unopened package, that contains the lighter, flints, wick, and a can of the fluid. The fluid is volatile and will evaporate over time, so in my trunk I keep a can of the fluid and only fill my 'emergency' zippo with the fluid as I leave the car.

6

MUST HAVE ESSENTIALS FOR A GET HOME BAG

A get home bag is not built for comfort or long term survival. Its sole function is to get you home as quickly as possible with as little drama as possible.

As noted survivalist Mors Kochanski[1] says, "The more you know the less you carry." If you have skills, then your bag can be smaller.

Like military line gear, the things you keep on your person everyday can help you in a disaster evacuation situation. Some, like myself, work in a place which limits every day carry items, you may not be.

Because I work in a prison, the only items I can constantly plan on having is a small P-38 military can opener on my keychain. Everything else must stay in my car. I am also limited on what can be in the car. Obviously, I cannot keep a long gun like an AR-15 in my car on prison grounds.

Earlier I mentioned why I believe typical long guns do not have a place in a basic get home bag setup.

For those that have better options for everyday carry, I set up a list of lists[2] on good everyday carry items for various types of people. I even have a list for those in non-permissive environments that don't allow weapons.

What is Important Now

I have a car kit in the event my vehicle breaks down. During normal situations, if I cannot fix it, I call my wife so she doesn't worry and I call a tow truck. I don't need much besides basic tools, and maybe some water.

If there is some type of disaster, everything changes. I need a plan, a means to get home, and a way to communicate with my wife.

Get Home Bag Content Checklist

I have a page with links[3] to various examples of items n this list, and can recommend all the items on that list as being a good value or a particularly good item.

As mentioned before, I like a modular kit, so not everything on this list is to be carried if the vehicle is left, but everything on this list has a purpose in the event you are stranded and either need to get help or walk home.

This is what I have in mine, feel free to add or delete as you find necessary

Car Recovery and Basic Repair

- Large rectangular Milk Crate
- Wool Blanket
- Watch Cap and Gloves
- Emergency Roadside Toolkit with tow strap, shovel, jumper cables, and basic tools
- Emergency LED Road Flares
- 12volt Portable Air Compressor
- Jack and 4 way lug wrench
- Come-along portable winch
- Road Atlas (preferably with topographical maps)
- Set of 4-33.75 Oz Glass Bottles with Stopper Caps filled with water
- Gallon of Oil
- 2 Gallons pre-mixed antifreeze
- Large contractor garbage bags

Basic Get Home Bag Kit

- Hydration Backpack
- 3 Day supply of Datrex 3600 Calorie Food Bars
- Camping tarp with lines and stakes
- Ultralight ground tarp
- Ultralight Sleeping Bag
- Ultralight Backpacking first aid kit
- Portable Water Filter Pump
- Titanium mug/pot
- Multi-tool
- Air Force Survival Knife
- Zippo All in One Kit
- 100 Feet Paracord
- Hooded Rain Jacket
- Emergency Headlamp

- Handheld CB radio (Marine is better, but less legal day to day)
- 100% Deet insect repellant
- Compass and maps for area
- Wool Hiking socks (2 pair)
- Good broken in Hiking boots
- Change of sturdy clothes, non-cotton.

I also keep a 9mm Glock 19 and 5 magazines in my kit, as well as a tinker model Swiss army knife and a Bic lighter in my glove compartment as well as a a mag-light.

My truck has more tools in it, my wife's car has less.

Your milage may vary, but you aren't fighting World War Three or Zombies. If you try to carry too much you will wish you had not tried to backpack with the kitchen sink.

ADDITIONAL RESOURCES

I wanted to keep this document short, an easy first-steps guide, but if you are interested in learning more I have included links to free articles from my site that are related to the concepts you have read about here:

- **Why Have a Personal Preparedness Mindset**
- **Why We Prepare**
- **Dealing with Family that Doesn't Understand Emergency Preparedness**
- **$10 Weekly Food Storage Program**
- **Introduction to Emergency Kits**
- **Bulk Food Storage Using Mylar Bags**
- **Water Storage**
- **DIY Bucket Water Filter**
- **Pool Shock for Water Purification**
- **Firearm Safety**
- **Firearms for Catastrophic Disasters**
- **Should You Shoot to Wound or to Kill?**
- **Communications Plan**

AFTERWORD

If prepping makes your life difficult, then you are not doing it right.

Prepping is life insurance, it is common sense, and it should make you sleep easier at night.

I sincerely hope you have learned something from this small booklet, and that it has given you information that will cause you to take additional steps toward self-reliance.

NOTES

1. Introduction

1. https://shepherdpublish.com/self-published-works/21-days-to-basic-preparedness/

2. Personal Preparedness Mindset

1. https://www.tngun.com/completed-incremental-disaster-kit/

3. Types of Emergency Kits

1. https://www.tngun.com/prn-40-alphabet-kits/

6. Must Have Essentials for a Get Home Bag

1. https://en.wikipedia.org/wiki/Mors_Kochanski
2. https://www.tngun.com/list-of-edc-lists/
3. https://www.tngun.com/essential-gear-for-a-get-home-bag/

PLEASE REVIEW

Please visit my Amazon Author Page at:

https://amazon.com/author/davidnash

if you like my work, you can really help me by publishing a review on Amazon.

The link to review this work at Amazon is:

https://www.amazon.com/review/create-review?asin=B07WPLBPZG

BONUS: EXCERPT FROM 21 DAYS TO BASIC PREPAREDNESS

There are quite a few schools of thought when it comes to personal disaster preparedness. The largest seems to be concerned with "Stuff". I call this the government model. In this model, practitioners buy gear to solve problems. They seem to feel that money equals solutions.

While you do need to have some level of resources, I feel this is a mistake, because stuff can get stolen, damaged, or lost. If you rely solely on gear, then no matter how redundant you think you are, you still have a single point of failure.

I believe in a balanced approach. In this document, I will illustrate basic concepts for disaster preparedness as well as give you some solid tips and steps to help you begin to prepare.

There is very little in the way of gear acquisition written in the following pages. You will need to acquire some measure of food, water, and equipment if you are to become more disaster resilient, however, there are multitudes of resources on and off line to help you do just that.

What is this book is designed to do is to guide you through the first steps of personal preparedness, i.e., "getting your mind right". I find that without a solid set of guideposts, it is easy to fall down the rabbit hole and concentrate only on buying stuff, or gaining training. Both of which are necessary, but neither will allow you the flexibility to adapt, improvise, or overcome.

Venn diagram of the relationship between skills, stuff, and training

I want you to be balanced, to have the right mix of things *and* skills with a strong mindset to be able to thrive in any situation.

I do not have all the answers, but I have spent decade's figuring out the best solutions for my family. Everything I wrote here are things I have done, and it has worked well for me. Take it as a guide and a starting point, question everything, and find your own solutions.

I have taken the liberty of writing this as if we were sitting in your living room talking; it is informal because preparedness does not have to be stressful.

Please do not mistake my familiar terms for ignorance of the subject. I have a degree in Emergency Management, hold certification as Emergency Management Professional, and have over a decade in planning and teaching Emergency Management in state service as well as a lifetime of doing this with my family.

If you like this Introduction to 21 Days to Basic Preparedness, you can find it on Amazon.

ALSO BY DAVID NASH

Fiction

The Deserter: Legion Chronicles Book 1

The Revolution: Legion Chronicles Book 2

The Return: Legion Chronicles Book 3

The Warrior: Legion Chronicles Book 4

Homestead Basics

The Basics of Raising Backyard Chickens

The Basics of Raising Backyard Rabbits

The Basics of Beginning Beekeeping

The Basics of Making Homemade Cheese

The Basics of Making Homemade Wine and Vinegar

The Basics of Making Homemade Cleaning Supplies

The Basics of Baking

The Basics of Food Preservation

The Basics of Food Storage

The Basics of Cooking Meat

The Basics of Make Ahead Mixes

The Basics of Beginning Leatherwork

Non Fiction

21 Days to Basic Preparedness

52 Prepper Projects

52 Prepper Projects for Parents and Kids

52 Unique Techniques for Stocking Food for Preppers

Basic Survival: A Beginner's Guide

Building a Get Home Bag

Handguns for Self Defense

How I Built a Ferrocement "Boulder Bunker"

New Instructor Survival Guide

The Prepper's Guide to Foraging

The Prepper's Guide to Foraging: Revised 2nd Edition

The Ultimate Guide to Pepper Spray

Understanding the Use of Handguns for Self Defense

Note and Record Books

Correction Officer's Notebook

Get Healthy Notebook

Rabbitry Records

Collections and Box Sets

Preparedness Collection

Legion Chronicles Trilogy

Translations

La Guía Definitiva Para El Spray De Pimienta

Multimedia

Alternative Energy

Firearm Manuals

Military Manuals 2 Disk Set

ABOUT THE AUTHOR

 David Nash is a former Marine with over a decade of experience in Emergency Management and another ten years in Corrections. He currently works in training as an instructor at a correction academy teaching new officers how to handle angry felons.

Add in a couple of semesters working in a liquor store during college and he has seen it all. In fact, David had the third highest prepper score on the NatGeo show Doomsday Preppers as well as worked more than 20 Presidentially declared disasters.

He has authored several books on preparedness, as well as worked on several disaster response plans as a state planner.

He is a father and a husband. He enjoys time with his young son William Tell and his school teacher wife Genny. When not working, writing, creating content for YouTube, playing on his self-reliance blog, or smoking award-winning BBQ he is asleep.

amazon.com/author/davidnash

facebook.com/booksbynash

youtube.com//tngun

goodreads.com/david_allen_nash

twitter.com/dnash1974

instagram.com/shepherdschool

pinterest.com/tngun